In case of loss, please return to:

_____

_____

_____

_____

As a reward: $ _____

Planning

event	date	notes

event	date	notes

Film Festivals

Africa	· Cairo International Film Festival (CIFF) - Cairo (Egypt) · Dockanema: Documentary Film Festival - Maputo (Mozambique) · Festival Panafricain du Cinéma et de la Télévision de Ouagadougou (FESPACO) - Ouagadougou (Burkina Faso)
North and Central America	· Ann Arbor Film Festival - Ann Arbor (Michigan, USA) · Chicago International Children's Film Festival (CICFF) - Chicago (Illinois, USA) · Dominican International Film Festival – Puerto Plata (Dominican Republic) · Environmental Film Festival at Yale - New Haven (Connecticut, USA) · Expresión en Corto International Film Festival - San Miguel de Allende and Guanajuato (Mexico) · Hollywood Film Festival - Los Angeles (California, USA) · Hot Docs: Canadian International Documentary Festival – Toronto (Canada) · International Film Festival in Guadalajara (FICG) - Guadalajara (Mexico) · New York Asian Film Festival (NYAFF) - New York City (New York, USA) · New York Film Festival (NYFF) - New York City (New York, USA) · Ottawa International Animation Festival – Ottawa (Canada) · San Francisco International Film Festival - San Francisco (California, USA) · Seattle International Film Festival (SIFF) - Seattle (Washington, USA) · Sonoma International Film Festival - Sonoma (California, USA) · South by Southwest (SXSW) - Austin (Texas, USA) · Sundance Film Festival - Park City, Salt Lake City, Ogden, Sundance (Utah, USA) · Telluride Film Festival - Telluride (Colorado, USA) · Titular Head - Grinnell (Iowa, USA) · Toronto International Film Festival (TIFF) - Toronto (Canada) · Tribeca Film Festival - New York City (New York, USA) · World Film Festival - Montreal (Canada)
South America	· Anima Mundi: International Animation Festival of Brazil - Rio de Janeiro and São Paulo (Brazil) · Festival de Cinema de Gramado - Gramado (Brazil) · Festival Internacional de Cine de Cartagena de Indias - Cartagena de Indias (Colombia) · Mar del Plata International Film Festival - Mar del Plata (Argentina) · Valdivia International Film Festival - Valdivia (Chile)
Asia	· Ahmedabad International Film Festival - Ahmedabad (India) · Con-Can Movie Festival - Tokyo (Japan) · Dubai International Film Festival - Dubai (United Arab Emirates)

· Hiroshima International Animation Festival - Hiroshima (Japan)
· International Film Festival of India (IFFI) - Goa (India)
· International Haifa Film Festival - Haifa (Israel)
· KaraFilm Festival: Karachi International Film Festival - Karachi (Pakistan)
· Kolkata Film Festival - Kolkata (India)
· Lahore International Children's Film Festival - Lahore (Pakistan)
· Mumbai Film Festival - Mumbai (India)
· Pusan International Film Festival - Pusan (South Korea)
· Shanghai International Film Festival - Shanghai (China)
· Taipei Golden Horse Film Festival - Taipei (Taiwan)
· Tokyo International Film Festival (TIFF) - Tokyo (Japan)

Europe

· Africa in Motion: Edinburgh African Film Festival (AiM) - Edinburgh (Scotland)
· Annecy International Animation Film Festival – Annecy (France)
· Berlinale - Berlin (Germany)
· Deauville American Film Festival - Deauville (France)
· Edinburgh International Film Festival - Edinburgh (Scotland)
· Encounters Short Film Festival - Bristol (England)
· Festival de Cannes - Cannes (France)
· Giffoni Experience - Giffoni Valle Piana (Italy)
· International İstanbul Film Festival – Istanbul (Turkey)
· International Rome Film Festival – Rome (Italy)
· Karlovy Vary International Film Festival - Karlovy Vary (Czech Republic)
· Krok: International Animated Films Festival – on a cruise ship, in Russia on even years (along the Volga) and Ukraine on odd years (along the Dnieper and the Black Sea)
· Locarno Film Festival - Locarno (Switzerland)
· Milano Film Festival – Milan (Italy)
· Moscow International Film Festival (MIFF) - Moscow (Russia)
· San Sebastian International Film Festival - San Sebastian (Spain)
· The Times BFI London Film Festival - London (England)
· Torino Film Festival (TFF) – Turin (Italy)
· Venice Film Festival - Venice (Italy)
· Zagreb Film Festival (ZFF) – Zagreb (Croatia)

Oceania

· Human Rights Arts and Film Festival - Melbourne, Sydney, Perth, Brisbane, Canberra (Australia)

Others

Film Journal

title

country · year

title in original language

genre

director

awards

starring

quotes

when · where · with

opinion

notes

rating ☆☆☆☆☆

country · year	title

genre	title in original language

awards	director

	starring

when · where · with	quotes

notes	opinion

rating ☆☆☆☆☆

title

country · year

title in original language

genre

director

awards

starring

quotes

when · where · with

opinion

notes

rating ☆☆☆☆☆

country · year

title

genre

title in original language

awards

director

starring

when · where · with

quotes

notes

opinion

rating ☆☆☆☆☆

title

country · year

title in original language

genre

director

awards

starring

quotes

when · where · with

opinion

notes

rating ☆☆☆☆☆

country · year	**title**
genre	title in original language
awards	director
	starring
when · where · with	quotes
notes	opinion

rating ☆☆☆☆☆

title

country · year

title in original language

genre

director

awards

starring

quotes

when · where · with

opinion

notes

rating ☆☆☆☆☆

country · year	title
genre	title in original language
awards	director
	starring
when · where · with	quotes
notes	opinion

rating ☆☆☆☆☆

15

title	country · year

title in original language	genre

director	awards

starring	

quotes	when · where · with

opinion	notes

rating ☆☆☆☆☆

country · year	title
genre	title in original language
awards	director
	starring
when · where · with	quotes
notes	opinion

rating ☆☆☆☆☆

title

country · year

title in original language

genre

director

awards

starring

quotes

when · where · with

opinion

notes

rating ☆☆☆☆☆

country · year	title
genre	title in original language
awards	director
	starring
when · where · with	quotes
notes	opinion

rating ☆☆☆☆☆

title

country · year

title in original language

genre

director

awards

starring

quotes

when · where · with

opinion

notes

rating ☆☆☆☆☆

country · year	title
genre	title in original language
awards	director
	starring
when · where · with	quotes
notes	opinion

rating ☆☆☆☆☆

title

country · year

title in original language

genre

director

awards

starring

quotes

when · where · with

opinion

notes

rating ☆☆☆☆☆

country · year	title

genre	title in original language

awards	director

	starring

when · where · with	quotes

notes	opinion

rating ☆☆☆☆☆

title

country · year

title in original language

genre

director

awards

starring

quotes

when · where · with

opinion

notes

rating ☆☆☆☆☆

country · year	title
genre	title in original language
awards	director
	starring
when · where · with	quotes
notes	opinion

rating ☆☆☆☆☆

title

country · year

title in original language

genre

director

awards

starring

quotes

when · where · with

opinion

notes

rating ☆☆☆☆☆

country · year	title

genre	title in original language

awards	director
	starring

when · where · with	quotes

notes	opinion

rating ☆☆☆☆☆

title

country · year

title in original language

genre

director

awards

starring

quotes

when · where · with

opinion

notes

rating ☆☆☆☆☆

country · year	title

genre	title in original language

awards	director

	starring

when · where · with	quotes

notes	opinion

rating ☆☆☆☆☆

title

country · year

title in original language

genre

director

awards

starring

quotes

when · where · with

opinion

notes

rating ☆☆☆☆☆

country · year	title

| genre | title in original language |

| awards | director |

| | starring |

| when · where · with | quotes |

| notes | opinion |

rating ☆☆☆☆☆

title

country · year

title in original language

genre

director

awards

starring

quotes

when · where · with

opinion

notes

rating ☆☆☆☆☆

country · year	**title**
genre	title in original language
awards	director
	starring
when · where · with	quotes
notes	opinion

rating ☆☆☆☆☆

title

country · year

title in original language

genre

director

awards

starring

quotes

when · where · with

opinion

notes

rating ☆☆☆☆☆

country · year

title

genre

title in original language

awards

director

starring

when · where · with

quotes

notes

opinion

rating ☆☆☆☆☆

title

country · year

title in original language

genre

director

awards

starring

quotes

when · where · with

opinion

notes

rating ☆☆☆☆☆

country · year	**title**
genre	title in original language
awards	director
	starring
when · where · with	quotes
notes	opinion

rating ☆☆☆☆☆

title

country · year

title in original language

genre

director

awards

starring

quotes

when · where · with

opinion

notes

rating ☆☆☆☆☆

country · year	title

genre	title in original language

awards	director

	starring

when · where · with	quotes

notes	opinion

rating ☆☆☆☆☆

title

country · year

title in original language

genre

director

awards

starring

quotes

when · where · with

opinion

notes

rating ☆☆☆☆☆

country · year

title

genre

title in original language

awards

director

starring

when · where · with

quotes

notes

opinion

rating ☆☆☆☆☆

title

country · year

title in original language

genre

director

awards

starring

quotes

when · where · with

opinion

notes

rating ☆☆☆☆☆

country · year	title
genre	title in original language
awards	director
	starring
when · where · with	quotes
notes	opinion

rating ☆ ☆ ☆ ☆ ☆

title

country · year

title in original language

genre

director

awards

starring

quotes

when · where · with

opinion

notes

rating ☆☆☆☆☆

44

country · year	title

genre	title in original language

awards	director

	starring

when · where · with	quotes

notes	opinion

rating ☆☆☆☆☆

title

country · year

title in original language

genre

director

awards

starring

quotes

when · where · with

opinion

notes

rating ☆☆☆☆☆

46

country · year

title

genre

title in original language

awards

director

starring

when · where · with

quotes

notes

opinion

rating ☆☆☆☆☆

title

country · year

title in original language

genre

director

awards

starring

quotes

when · where · with

opinion

notes

rating ☆☆☆☆☆

48

country · year

title

genre

title in original language

awards

director

starring

when · where · with

quotes

notes

opinion

rating ☆☆☆☆☆

title

country · year

title in original language

genre

director

awards

starring

quotes

when · where · with

opinion

notes

rating ☆☆☆☆☆

country · year	title

genre	title in original language

awards	director

	starring

when · where · with	quotes

notes	opinion

rating ☆☆☆☆☆

title

country · year

title in original language

genre

director

awards

starring

quotes

when · where · with

opinion

notes

rating ☆☆☆☆☆

52

country · year	**title**
genre	title in original language
awards	director
	starring
when · where · with	quotes
notes	opinion

rating ☆☆☆☆☆

title

country · year

title in original language

genre

director

awards

starring

quotes

when · where · with

opinion

notes

rating ☆☆☆☆☆

country · year	title
genre	title in original language
awards	director
	starring
when · where · with	quotes
notes	opinion

rating ☆☆☆☆☆

title

country · year

title in original language

genre

director

awards

starring

quotes

when · where · with

opinion

notes

rating ☆☆☆☆☆

country · year	title
genre	title in original language
awards	director
	starring
when · where · with	quotes
notes	opinion

rating ☆☆☆☆☆

title

country · year

title in original language

genre

director

awards

starring

quotes

when · where · with

opinion

notes

rating ☆☆☆☆☆

country · year	title
genre	title in original language
awards	director
	starring
when · where · with	quotes
notes	opinion
	rating ☆☆☆☆☆

title

country · year

title in original language

genre

director

awards

starring

quotes

when · where · with

opinion

notes

rating ☆☆☆☆☆

60

country · year	title
genre	title in original language
awards	director
	starring
when · where · with	quotes
notes	opinion

rating ☆☆☆☆☆

title

country · year

title in original language

genre

director

awards

starring

quotes

when · where · with

opinion

notes

rating ☆☆☆☆☆

country · year	title
genre	title in original language
awards	director
	starring
when · where · with	quotes
notes	opinion

rating ☆☆☆☆☆

title

country · year

title in original language

genre

director

awards

starring

quotes

when · where · with

opinion

notes

rating ☆☆☆☆☆

country · year	title
genre	title in original language
awards	director
	starring
when · where · with	quotes
notes	opinion

rating ☆☆☆☆☆

title

country · year

title in original language

genre

director

awards

starring

quotes

when · where · with

opinion

notes

rating ☆☆☆☆☆

country · year	title
genre	title in original language
awards	director
	starring
when · where · with	quotes
notes	opinion

rating ☆☆☆☆☆

title

country · year

title in original language

genre

director

awards

starring

quotes

when · where · with

opinion

notes

rating ☆☆☆☆☆

country · year

title

genre

title in original language

awards

director

starring

when · where · with

quotes

notes

opinion

rating ☆☆☆☆☆

title

country · year

title in original language

genre

director

awards

starring

quotes

when · where · with

opinion

notes

rating ☆☆☆☆☆

70

country · year	title
genre	title in original language
awards	director
	starring
when · where · with	quotes
notes	opinion

rating ☆☆☆☆☆

title

country · year

title in original language

genre

director

awards

starring

quotes

when · where · with

opinion

notes

rating ☆☆☆☆☆

country · year	title
genre	title in original language
awards	director
	starring
when · where · with	quotes
notes	opinion

rating ☆☆☆☆☆

title	country · year

title in original language	genre

director	awards

starring

quotes	when · where · with

L

opinion	notes

rating ☆☆☆☆☆

74

country · year	title

genre · title in original language

awards · director

starring

when · where · with · quotes

notes · opinion

rating ☆☆☆☆☆

title

country · year

title in original language

genre

director

awards

starring

quotes

when · where · with

opinion

notes

rating ☆☆☆☆☆

country · year | title

genre | title in original language

awards | director

starring

when · where · with | quotes

notes | opinion

rating ☆☆☆☆☆

title

country · year

title in original language

genre

director

awards

starring

quotes

when · where · with

opinion

notes

rating ☆☆☆☆☆

country · year	title

genre	title in original language

awards	director

	starring

when · where · with	quotes

notes	opinion

rating ☆☆☆☆☆

title

country · year

title in original language

genre

director

awards

starring

quotes

when · where · with

opinion

notes

rating ☆☆☆☆☆

country · year	title

genre	title in original language

awards	director

	starring

when · where · with	quotes

notes	opinion

rating ☆☆☆☆☆

title

country · year

title in original language

genre

director

awards

starring

quotes

when · where · with

opinion

notes

rating ☆☆☆☆☆

country · year

title

genre

title in original language

awards

director

starring

when · where · with

quotes

notes

opinion

rating ☆☆☆☆☆

title

country · year

title in original language

genre

director

awards

starring

quotes

when · where · with

opinion

notes

rating ☆☆☆☆☆

country · year

title

genre

title in original language

awards

director

starring

when · where · with

quotes

notes

opinion

rating ☆☆☆☆☆

title

country · year

title in original language

genre

director

awards

starring

quotes

when · where · with

opinion

notes

rating ☆☆☆☆☆

country · year

title

genre

title in original language

awards

director

starring

when · where · with

quotes

notes

opinion

rating ☆☆☆☆☆

title

country · year

title in original language

genre

director

awards

starring

quotes

when · where · with

opinion

notes

rating ☆☆☆☆☆

country · year	title

genre	title in original language

awards	director

	starring

when · where · with	quotes

notes	opinion

rating ☆☆☆☆☆

title

country · year

title in original language

genre

director

awards

starring

quotes

when · where · with

opinion

notes

rating ☆☆☆☆☆

90

country · year	title

| genre | title in original language |

| awards | director |

| | starring |

| when · where · with | quotes |

| notes | opinion |

rating ☆☆☆☆☆

title

country · year

title in original language

genre

director

awards

starring

quotes

when · where · with

0

opinion

notes

rating ☆☆☆☆☆

country · year	title

genre   title in original language

awards   director

starring

when · where · with   quotes

notes   opinion

rating ☆☆☆☆☆

title

country · year

title in original language

genre

director

awards

starring

quotes

when · where · with

opinion

notes

rating ☆☆☆☆☆

country · year

title

genre

title in original language

awards

director

starring

when · where · with

quotes

notes

opinion

rating ☆☆☆☆☆

title

country · year

title in original language

genre

director

awards

starring

quotes

when · where · with

opinion

notes

rating ☆☆☆☆☆

country · year

title

genre

title in original language

awards

director

starring

when · where · with

quotes

notes

opinion

rating ☆☆☆☆☆

| title | country · year |

title in original language — genre

director — awards

starring

quotes — when · where · with

P

opinion — notes

rating ☆☆☆☆☆

country · year	title

genre	title in original language

awards	director

	starring

when · where · with	quotes

notes	opinion

rating ☆☆☆☆☆

title

country · year

title in original language

genre

director

awards

starring

quotes

when · where · with

opinion

notes

rating ☆☆☆☆☆

country · year	title

genre	title in original language

awards	director
	starring

when · where · with	quotes

notes	opinion

rating ☆☆☆☆☆

title

country · year

title in original language

genre

director

awards

starring

quotes

when · where · with

opinion

notes

rating ☆☆☆☆☆

country · year

title

genre

title in original language

awards

director

starring

when · where · with

quotes

notes

opinion

rating ☆☆☆☆☆

title

country · year

title in original language

genre

director

awards

starring

quotes

when · where · with

opinion

notes

Q

rating ☆☆☆☆☆

country · year	title

genre	title in original language

awards	director

	starring

when · where · with	quotes

notes	opinion

rating ☆☆☆☆☆

title

country · year

title in original language

genre

director

awards

starring

quotes

when · where · with

opinion

notes

rating ☆☆☆☆☆

country · year	**title**
genre	title in original language
awards	director
	starring
when · where · with	quotes
notes	opinion

rating ☆☆☆☆☆

title

country · year

title in original language

genre

director

awards

starring

quotes

when · where · with

opinion

notes

rating ☆☆☆☆☆

country · year	title
genre	title in original language
awards	director
	starring
when · where · with	quotes
notes	opinion

rating ☆☆☆☆☆

title

country · year

title in original language

genre

director

awards

starring

quotes

when · where · with

opinion

notes

R

rating ☆☆☆☆☆

country · year | title

genre | title in original language

awards | director

starring

when · where · with | quotes

notes | opinion

rating ☆☆☆☆☆

title

country · year

title in original language

genre

director

awards

starring

quotes

when · where · with

opinion

notes

rating ☆☆☆☆☆

country · year	title

genre	title in original language

awards	director

	starring

when · where · with	quotes

notes	opinion

rating ☆☆☆☆☆

title

country · year

title in original language

genre

director

awards

starring

quotes

when · where · with

opinion

notes

rating ☆☆☆☆☆

114

country · year	title

genre	title in original language

awards	director

starring

when · where · with	quotes

notes	opinion

rating ☆☆☆☆☆

title

country · year

title in original language

genre

director

awards

starring

quotes

when · where · with

opinion

notes

S

rating ☆☆☆☆☆

116

country · year

title

genre

title in original language

awards

director

starring

when · where · with

quotes

notes

opinion

rating ☆☆☆☆☆

title

country · year

title in original language

genre

director

awards

starring

quotes

when · where · with

opinion

notes

rating ☆☆☆☆☆

country · year	title

genre	title in original language

awards	director

	starring

when · where · with	quotes

notes	opinion

rating ☆☆☆☆☆

title

country · year

title in original language

genre

director

awards

starring

quotes

when · where · with

opinion

notes

rating ☆☆☆☆☆

120

country · year	title

genre	title in original language

awards	director

	starring

when · where · with	quotes

notes	opinion

rating ☆☆☆☆☆

title

country · year

title in original language

genre

director

awards

starring

quotes

when · where · with

opinion

notes

T

rating ☆☆☆☆☆

country · year	title
genre	title in original language
awards	director
	starring
when · where · with	quotes
notes	opinion

rating ☆☆☆☆☆

title

country · year

title in original language

genre

director

awards

starring

quotes

when · where · with

opinion

notes

rating ☆☆☆☆☆

country · year	**title**
genre	title in original language
awards	director
	starring
when · where · with	quotes
notes	opinion

rating ☆☆☆☆☆

title

country · year

title in original language

genre

director

awards

starring

quotes

when · where · with

opinion

notes

rating ☆☆☆☆☆

country · year	title

genre	title in original language

awards	director

	starring

when · where · with	quotes

notes	opinion

rating ☆☆☆☆☆

title

country · year

title in original language

genre

director

awards

starring

quotes

when · where · with

opinion

notes

rating ☆☆☆☆☆

U

country · year	title

genre	title in original language

awards	director

	starring

when · where · with	quotes

notes	opinion

rating ☆☆☆☆☆

title

country · year

title in original language

genre

director

awards

starring

quotes

when · where · with

opinion

notes

rating ☆☆☆☆☆

130

country · year

title

genre

title in original language

awards

director

starring

when · where · with

quotes

notes

opinion

rating ☆☆☆☆☆

title

country · year

title in original language

genre

director

awards

starring

quotes

when · where · with

opinion

notes

rating ☆☆☆☆☆

country · year	title

genre	title in original language

awards	director

starring

when · where · with	quotes

notes	opinion

rating ☆☆☆☆☆

title

country · year

title in original language

genre

director

awards

starring

quotes

when · where · with

opinion

notes

rating ☆☆☆☆☆

V

country · year	title

| genre | title in original language |

| awards | director |

| | starring |

| when · where · with | quotes |

| notes | opinion |

rating ☆☆☆☆☆

135

title

country · year

title in original language

genre

director

awards

starring

quotes

when · where · with

opinion

notes

rating ☆☆☆☆☆

country · year	title

genre	title in original language

awards	director

	starring

when · where · with	quotes

notes	opinion

rating ☆☆☆☆☆

title

country · year

title in original language

genre

director

awards

starring

quotes

when · where · with

opinion

notes

rating ☆☆☆☆☆

country · year

title

genre

title in original language

awards

director

starring

when · where · with

quotes

notes

opinion

rating ☆☆☆☆☆

title

country · year

title in original language

genre

director

awards

starring

quotes

when · where · with

opinion

notes

rating ☆☆☆☆☆

W

140

country · year

title

genre

title in original language

awards

director

starring

when · where · with

quotes

notes

opinion

rating ☆☆☆☆☆

title

country · year

title in original language

genre

director

awards

starring

quotes

when · where · with

opinion

notes

rating ☆☆☆☆☆

country · year	title

genre	title in original language

awards	director

starring

when · where · with	quotes

notes	opinion

rating ☆☆☆☆☆

title

country · year

title in original language

genre

director

awards

starring

quotes

when · where · with

opinion

notes

rating ☆☆☆☆☆

country · year	title
genre	title in original language
awards	director
	starring
when · where · with	quotes
notes	opinion

rating ☆☆☆☆☆

title

country · year

title in original language

genre

director

awards

starring

quotes

when · where · with

opinion

notes

rating ☆☆☆☆☆

X

country · year	title
genre	title in original language
awards	director
	starring
when · where · with	quotes
notes	opinion

rating ☆☆☆☆☆

title

country · year

title in original language

genre

director

awards

starring

quotes

when · where · with

opinion

notes

rating ☆☆☆☆☆

148

country · year	title

| genre | title in original language |

| awards | director |

| | starring |

| when · where · with | quotes |

| notes | opinion |

rating ☆☆☆☆☆

title

country · year

title in original language

genre

director

awards

starring

quotes

when · where · with

opinion

notes

rating ☆☆☆☆☆

country · year

title

genre

title in original language

awards

director

starring

when · where · with

quotes

notes

opinion

rating ☆☆☆☆☆

title

country · year

title in original language

genre

director

awards

starring

quotes

when · where · with

opinion

notes

rating ☆☆☆☆☆

Y

country · year

title

genre

title in original language

awards

director

starring

when · where · with

quotes

notes

opinion

rating ☆☆☆☆☆

---

title

country · year

title in original language

genre

director

awards

starring

quotes

when · where · with

opinion

notes

rating ☆☆☆☆☆

154

country · year	title

genre	title in original language

awards	director

	starring

when · where · with	quotes

notes	opinion

rating ☆☆☆☆☆

title

country · year

title in original language

genre

director

awards

starring

quotes

when · where · with

opinion

notes

rating ☆☆☆☆☆

156

country · year	title

genre	title in original language

awards	director

	starring

when · where · with	quotes

notes	opinion

rating ☆☆☆☆☆

title

country · year

title in original language

genre

director

awards

starring

quotes

when · where · with

opinion

notes

rating ☆☆☆☆☆

Z

country · year

title

genre

title in original language

awards

director

starring

when · where · with

quotes

notes

opinion

rating ☆☆☆☆☆

title

country · year

title in original language

genre

director

awards

starring

quotes

when · where · with

opinion

notes

rating ☆☆☆☆☆

country · year

title

genre

title in original language

awards

director

starring

when · where · with

quotes

notes

opinion

rating ☆☆☆☆☆

title

country · year

title in original language

genre

director

awards

starring

quotes

when · where · with

opinion

notes

rating ☆☆☆☆☆

185

221

Index